cats

20 jewelry and accessory designs

by Sian Hamilton

THE GUILD OF MASTER CRAFTSMAN
PUBLICATIONS

First published 2014 by
Guild of Master Craftsman Publications Ltd
Castle Place, 166 High Street, Lewes,
East Sussex BN7 1XU

Text © Sian Hamilton, 2014
Copyright in the Work © GMC Publications Ltd, 2014

ISBN 978 1 86108 944 1

A catalog record for this book is available
from the British Library.

Set in King and Myriad
Color origination by GMC Reprographics
Printed and bound in China

Publisher Jonathan Bailey
Production Manager Jim Bulley
Managing Editor Gerrie Purcell
Senior Project Editor Wendy McAngus
Editor Jane Roe
Managing Art Editor Gilda Pacitti
Cover Photograph Rebecca Mothersole
Photographer Andrew Perris
Designer Simon Goggin

MAL

Cumbria
County Council

Libraries, books and more . . .

MARYPORT		COCKERMOUTH
4 SEP 2014		
26 FEB 2015		

Please return/renew this item by the last due date.
Library items may be renewed by phone on
030 33 33 1234 (24 hours) or via our website
www.cumbria.gov.uk/libraries

Cumbria Libraries
CLIC
Interactive Catalogue

Ask for a CLIC password

contents

Continued...

CANDY

JINX

The Projects

POLLY

SAMBA

PADDY

OSCAR

COCO

GRACIE

LUNA

MOLLY

TRIGGER

AVALON

JASPER

KITTY

FELIX

STAR

ATHENA

MILO

LEO

NALA

Tools and equipment

pliers and cutters

ROUND-NOSE PLIERS

These pliers have round jaws that taper to the end. They are used for making jumprings, eyepins, loops, and spirals.

ROUND-NOSE PLIERS

CHAIN-NOSE PLIERS

Sometimes known as snipe-nose, these pliers have flat jaws that taper at the end. They are useful for holding small items such as neck ends and for opening and closing jumprings.

FLAT-NOSE PLIERS

These have flat jaws that do not taper. They are used for holding wire, closing ribbon crimps, and opening and closing jumprings.

SIDE CUTTERS

These cutters have the cutting jaw on the side; they have a pointed nose and can cut flush to your piece. The point also allows the cutters to access smaller areas.

SCISSORS

Small, sharp-pointed scissors are used for trimming cord, ribbon, thread, and cutting shrink plastic.

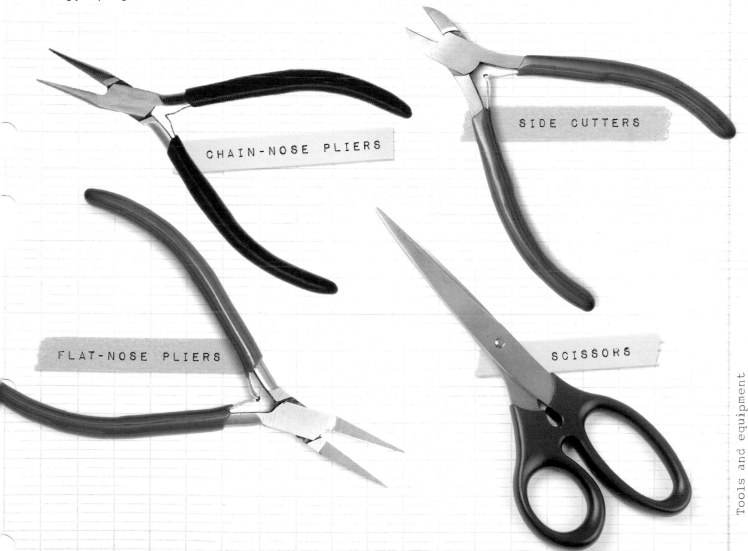

CHAIN-NOSE PLIERS

SIDE CUTTERS

FLAT-NOSE PLIERS

SCISSORS

Tools and equipment

miscellaneous tools

All of these tools are used in the projects in this book;
many of them are nonspecialist items available in
hardware and craft stores.

ADHESIVES

When making jewelry, use glues that are suited to the purpose. Many cyanoacrylate glues (also known as superglue) can react with metals and melt materials, so should only be used for certain tasks. PVA glue is a common glue that is often used when working with children; it is white in color and can be used to seal paper. GS Hypo Cement is a liquid glue and good for adding to knots for extra security. E6000 is industrial thick glue used to coat wire to stop sharp edges from scratching skin and for sticking shrink plastic to combs and metal findings. Use adhesives in a well-ventilated area.

TAPE MEASURE

A standard tape measure is an essential tool for measuring chain, cord, and ribbon, and for making sure the finished piece is the length you want.

BEAD MAT

These mats feel like velvet and have a texture that holds onto beads, stopping them from rolling around on the work surface and getting lost.

MANDRELS

These are useful for making rings and bangles. They come in a variety of sizes and shapes, in both plastic and metal.

ROLLERS

For use with polymer clay and metal clay, rollers are a hollow or solid plastic tube that you use to roll clays out to a thin sheet. You can make your own by cutting a small section of tubing that is widely available in building supplies stores in the plumbing aisle.

ADHESIVES

E-6000

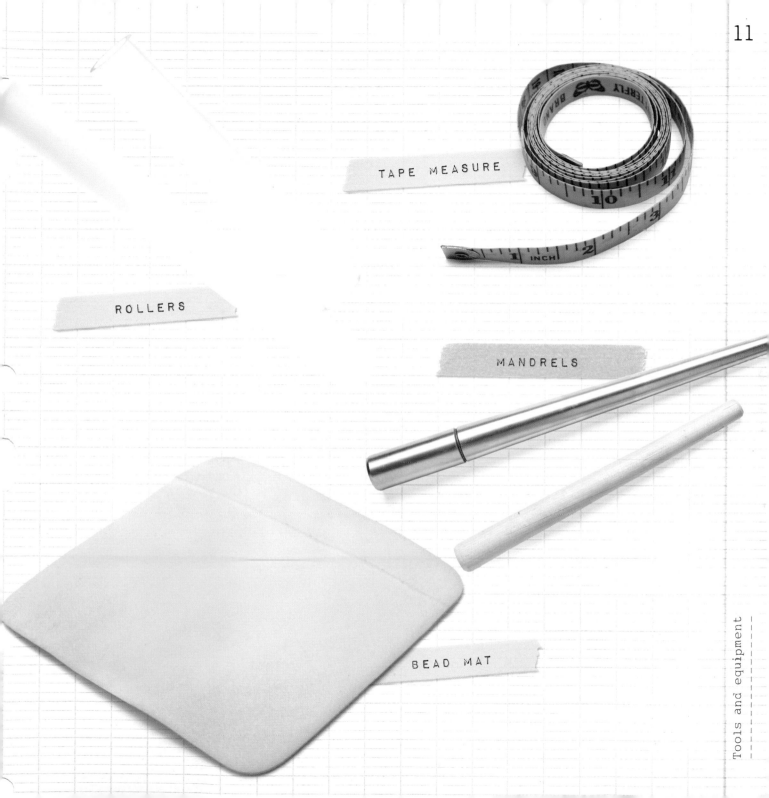

TAPE MEASURE

ROLLERS

MANDRELS

BEAD MAT

CUTTERS

Specialist cutters for polymer or resin clay are made from metal and come in a wide variety of shapes. Sugar craft cutters can also be used; made from plastic, they are cheaper and have a mechanism to push the clay out of the end.

SPACERS

Used to get a consistent thickness when rolling out clay, spacers are plastic bars that come in a set of different thicknesses. Put them either side of the clay while you roll it out. A stack of playing cards works just as well.

TEFLON SHEET

Sold in most cook stores, Teflon sheet is nonstick and is used to roll clay out on. It can be cut to size.

EMERY PAPER

Used to soften sharp edges on findings and wire or to smooth the edge of clay pieces. Specialist foam-backed emery paper holds its shape and works really well on clay.

STICKY TACK

This is malleable putty that is a reusable adhesive. Commonly used to stick posters to walls, it works well to help prop up jewelry pieces when using resin or when leaving something to dry that needs to be kept up in the air. It has a variety of names subject to brand.

MARKER PENS

Permanent marker pens come in a large variety of nibs and will write on most surfaces. If using them to mark measured points, remember to mark where it won't be seen on the finished piece of jewelry. They can be used on wooden beads to make a pattern that does not come off and even come in a variety of colors that work well with things like shrink plastic.

CUTTERS

SPACERS

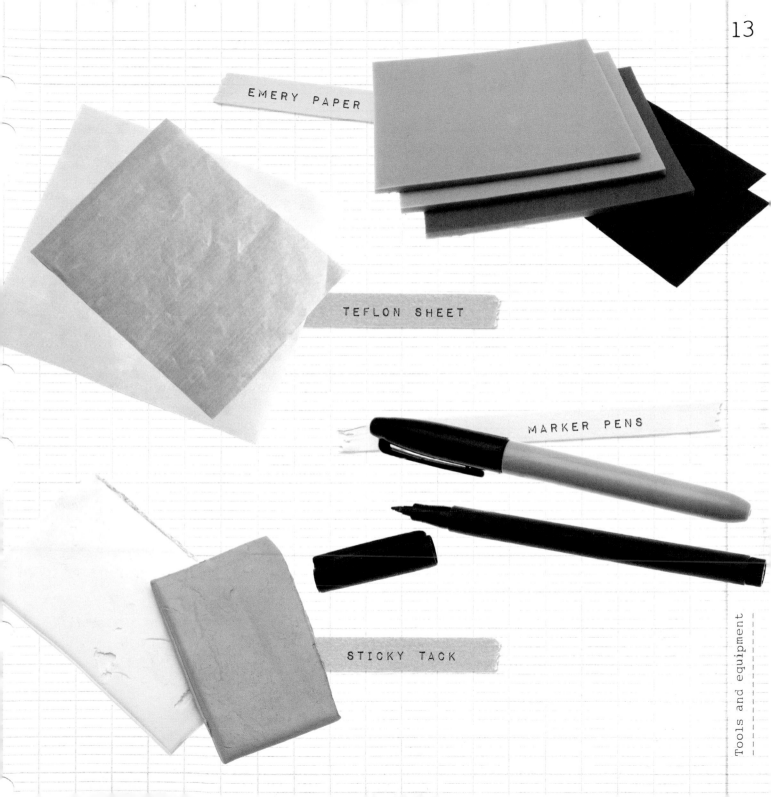

EMERY PAPER

TEFLON SHEET

MARKER PENS

STICKY TACK

Tools and equipment

Materials

SO YOU CAN HAVE FUN WITHOUT TOO MUCH EXPENSE THE
PROJECTS IN THIS BOOK ARE MADE USING MATERIALS
THAT ARE EASY TO FIND AND REASONABLY CHEAP.

embellishments

BEADS

There is such a large variety of beads available, from tiny seed beads to large, handmade lampwork glass ones. Beads can be made from plastic, wood, metal, glass, resin, or crystal. When selecting beads, it's good to start with a theme, such as cats, then match different styles of beads together using a color palette.

BEADS

CRYSTALS

Crystals come as beads, pendants, buttons, flat-back stones, and pointed-back stones (called chatons). They are beautiful and add sparkle to designs. Flat-back and chatons can be used with resin clay, or stuck on anything else with appropriate glue.

BUTTONS

Shaped buttons are great for jewelry as they come with premade holes to attach them to jumprings or wire.

CHARMS

Charms can be metal, plastic, wood, or pretty much any material. The term "charm" is often given to a jewelry item that has a hole or loop at the top to attach it to the jewelry.

BUTTONS

CRYSTALS

CHARMS

stringing materials

CHOKER

Ready-made necklaces are widely available; they come in different sizes and most have a screw clasp. The wire choker style is usually made from steel wire coated in nylon, which is then colored.

NYLON-COATED WIRE

A range of brands is available. This wire is really good for stringing, as it has a better strength for heavy beads than ordinary threads. It also holds a nice shape on the neck.

BEADING THREAD AND BEADING NEEDLE

These are used for seed beading and beadweaving. The thicker threads can be used for bead stringing and secured with calotte ends.

WIRE

Wire comes in a large range of sizes. Often referred to in the USA by gauge and in the UK by millimeters, conversion charts are widely available on the Internet. If buying plated wire, look for a non-tarnish variety.

CHOKER

NYLON-COATED WIRE

BEADING THREAD AND BEADING NEEDLE

other essentials

CHAIN

There are many styles of chain and a variety of colors available. Fine chains are good for hanging pendants and large-link chains are good for making charm bracelets or when adding beads to the individual links.

SHRINK PLASTIC

This is a paper-thin plastic that shrinks in a standard oven and becomes seven times smaller and seven times thicker than its original size. It can be colored and cut into any shape with scissors. You can also create shapes in it using paper punches.

POLYMER CLAY

Polymer clay is a plastic modeling compound that is soft and pliable until it is baked in a standard oven. It comes in a large variety of colors and brands; each brand has a different baking temperature, so check the manufacturer's instructions before using. Polymer clay also comes in great special effects, such as metallic colors and even one that glows in the dark!

POLYMER CLAY

CHAIN

SHRINK PLASTIC

WIRE

findings

Findings are all the items you use to make up jewelry
that are not beads, pendants, or charms.

EARWIRES

Earwires come in various styles, from a simple "U" shape with a loop, to ones with a bead and coil finish. The loop is opened to take the earring piece.

HEADPINS AND EYEPINS

These are pieces of wire with a flat or ball end (headpin) or a loop at the end (eyepin). Thread a bead on the wire and make a loop at the open end to secure the bead in place. Eyepins can be linked together to make a chain.

JUMPRINGS

A jumpring is a single ring of wire that is used to join pieces together; they come in every size you can think of and also in many colors.

POSTS AND BACKS

Posts come with a bead and open loop or with a blank disc front. The disc style is used with glue. They are often supplied with butterfly/scroll backs.

TRIGGER

These are also known as a lobster or parrot clasp. These are the most widely used clasps on the market. Some come with a jumpring attached and they vary in size and style.

EARWIRES

JUMPRINGS

HEADPINS AND EYEPINS

TRIGGER

POSTS AND BACKS

BOLT RING

The spring-closing mechanism in this pushes a bar across the opening. They are used in exactly the same way as a trigger clasp.

MAGNETIC

These are great for bracelets when making for anyone who finds opening and closing clasps difficult. Keep in mind that magnets will attach to some base metals like plated chains.

PUSH BUTTON

These clasps have a ball on one piece and a ring on the other; both sides have loops to attach to necklaces. The ball pushes through the ring and holds it closed, as it is slightly larger than the hole in the ring.

SCREW

This type of clasp is best suited to designs where the strung section can spin freely in the clasp or your piece will twist as you screw it on.

TOGGLE

A great choice when making the clasp a feature in your design, toggles have a loop on one end and a bar that fits through the loop to attach to the other end.

BOLT RING

SCREW

PUSH BUTTON

MAGNETIC

TOGGLE

BEAD CAPS

BROOCH AND BACK BAR

CALOTTES

Calottes are small hinged cups with a loop on one cup (these can be open loops or closed rings) and a hole in the middle of the hinge to take thread. They work by holding a seed bead or crimp bead inside the cup with the thread coming out of hole in the hinge to make the ends of piece look neater. To close them gently press the two cups together. The loop is for attaching the calotte to jumprings or clasps.

BEAD CAPS

These are slightly domed shapes with a hole in the center, which fit over the ends of beads to add extra decoration.

BROOCH BACK AND BAR

This is a brooch pin on a bar that has holes to attach it to the piece of jewelry. It can be sewn on, attached with wire, or glued.

HAIR COMBS

Clear combs are good for jewelry making as you can embellish them with wire and beads or glue a feature piece on the front.

TIARA BAND

Round tiara bands sit on top of the head or can be gently bent out to make a "U" shape for a hair band to sit behind the ears. They come in silver or gold colors and are made of a strip of metal.

CALOTTES

TIARA BAND

HAIR COMB

HAIR CLASPS

These clasps are usually made from metal and can be pushed open and then spring closed to grasp the hair. They are great for gluing things onto for simple hair accessories.

HAIR BARRETTE

Plain metal barrette bases can be bought from many jewelry findings suppliers. They come in a variety of sizes and can be decorated with beads and wire or by gluing a piece on the top.

BLANKS

These are pieces with a plate fixed to the top that you can glue decoration to. You can get blanks on ring shanks, cuff links, and as buttons.

BEZEL BLANKS

These are flat plates with a shallow wall around the sides, either with a loop on one end to attach to a chain or attached to cuff link backs, ring shanks, or bracelets. They can be filled with resin or clay. They come in a variety of shapes.

HAIR CLASPS

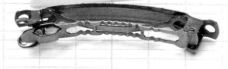

HAIR BARRETTE

BLANKS

BEZEL BLANKS

Techniques

THE FOLLOWING PAGES WILL ILLUSTRATE SOME OF THE BASIC TECHNIQUES NEEDED TO MAKE YOUR OWN JEWELRY AND COMPLETE THE PROJECTS IN THIS BOOK.

working with findings

Here is how to use and create some of the small components that make up your pieces of jewelry.

OPENING AND CLOSING A JUMPRING

To make sure that jumprings shut securely, it is important to know how to open and close them correctly.

1 Grip a jumpring in two pairs of pliers with the opening centered at the top.

2 Holding the jumping on both sides, twist one hand toward you while twisting the other hand away. This will keep the ring round in shape. Reverse the action to close the ring.

MAKING JUMPRINGS

1 Select a rod that is the right diameter for the jumprings you want to make (a knitting needle will work well). Wind the wire around the rod to make a coil. For most projects, US 20 gauge (SWG 21, 0.8mm) will be suitable for rings under 8mm; use larger wire for bigger jumprings. Keep the coil as tight as you can.

2 Take a pair of side cutters (if you can get semi-flush cutters they will give you the best results) and, with the flat side facing the coil, snip off the very end.

3 Now turn the cutters around so the flat side faces away from the main coil and snip the ring off the coil. Get the pliers as close to the cut end as possible so you achieve a full circle of wire.

4 When you have cut each ring off you'll notice the end looks bevelled, as in this image. You need to get rid of this bevelled edge to give your rings a straight edge so that they close well.

5 Turn the cutters again and snip off the very end of the coil (as in step 2), you will need to do this for each ring. This feels long-winded but it will make your jumprings look better in the long run. When cut, your rings should look like this one. To close the gap on the ring, hold in pliers as per the instructions for opening and closing jumprings on the following page, and wiggle the ring back and forth, pushing it gently together.

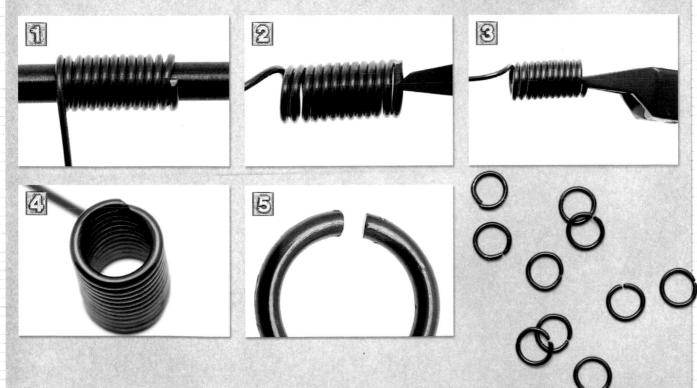

Techniques

CONDITIONING AND ROLLING OUT POLYMER CLAY

When using new polymer clay you will need to condition it. Get the clay out of the packet and squeeze it in your hands, then roll it flat with a roller, fold the sheet in half and roll flat again. Keep doing this until the clay is soft and malleable.

To roll clay into an even sheet use either spacers (see page 12) or playing cards. Place the clay on a non-stick surface such as Teflon sheet and flatten slightly with your hand. Place the spacers or cards either side of the clay, close enough that the roller can roll over the clay and spacers or cards. Roll with an even pressure until the clay is level with the spacers or cards.

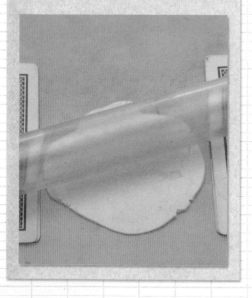

making simple and wrapped loops

Loops have a multitude of functions in jewelry so making them properly is a skill worth mastering.

HOW TO MAKE A SIMPLE LOOP

A simple (sometimes called open) loop can be opened and closed to allow it to be attached and detached as desired.

1   Thread your chosen bead onto a headpin or eyepin.

2   Bend the wire to a right angle against the bead.

3   Snip off to ³/₈in (8mm). Leave more wire if you need a big loop. Hold the end of the wire in round-nose pliers and roll back toward the bead to create the loop.

HOW TO MAKE A WRAPPED LOOP

This style of loop is the most secure; once attached it cannot be removed unless it is cut off.

1. Thread your chosen bead onto a headpin or eyepin.

2. Hold the pin against the bead with a pair of round-nose pliers and bend the wire above the pliers to a right angle.

3. Move the pliers to the top of the right angle and bend the wire all the way around the pliers until it sits by the bead.

4. Thread the loop you have made onto the component you are attaching it to, such as a chain.

5. Hold the loop in the round-nose pliers' jaws with the chain away from the bead and wrap the end of the pin around the stem above the bead.

6. Wrap around until the wire meets the bead and snip off any excess wire.

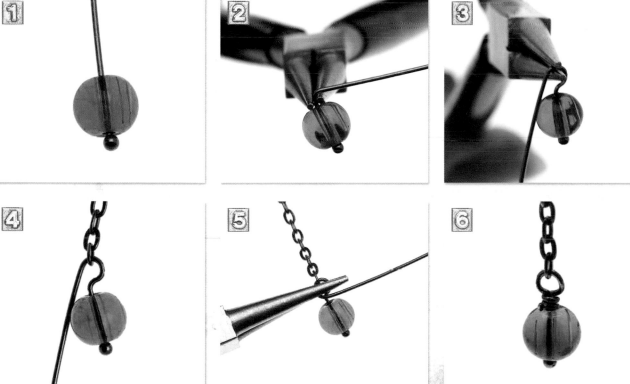

using shrink plastic

Shrink plastic is very easy to use and is a great way to get kids started on making their own unique jewelry.

SHRINKING THE PLASTIC

This type of plastic shrinks to become a rigid plastic about $\frac{1}{16}$ in (2mm) thick; this can vary by brand. The plastic can be shrunk in a standard kitchen oven, and is good for making simple shapes such as circles and squares. Place in the oven at a high temperature (around 350°F/175°C) and heat for about one minute. You will need to watch the plastic, as it will melt if left in the oven too long. Leave to cool before touching.

1 A craft heat gun is the best tool for the job if you have complicated shapes, as you can control how the plastic shrinks. If doing this with children, always have an adult use the gun.

2 Hold the plastic against a heat-resistant surface with a pair of heat-resistant tweezers. Holding the heat gun about 2in (50mm) from the plastic, heat the plastic until it begins to shrink. The shape will twist and fold in on itself.

3 Keep moving the heat gun over the plastic until it untwists and goes flat. Don't hold the gun in one place for too long as the plastic can melt. When the plastic has completely shrunk (when it stops moving and is fairly flat), get a flat-bottomed glass and, before the plastic goes cold, press it lightly to with the glass to completely flatten it. In the photograph you can see the difference in size before and after the plastic has been shrunk.

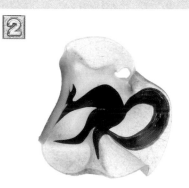

COLORING SHRINK PLASTIC

There are multiple ways of coloring the plastic, which is usually done before the shape is cut out of a sheet.

1   Draw the outline for your design on the matte side of the plastic. Make sure you use a pencil that will show up—white is a good color for dark-colored plastic and a standard drawing pencil works on a light or frosted sheet.

2   If you have a design that requires a pen outline, then use a permanent marker and draw on the shiny side.

3   The plastic can be colored with standard coloring pencils on the matte side. Children can simply draw straight onto the plastic sheet.

4   Inks can also be used to color shrink plastic, using either craft stamps or small sponges. Always apply a light coat of ink, as the color will intensify when shrunk.

5   Cut around the design with small sharp scissors or use a craft punch to create simple shapes such as circles.

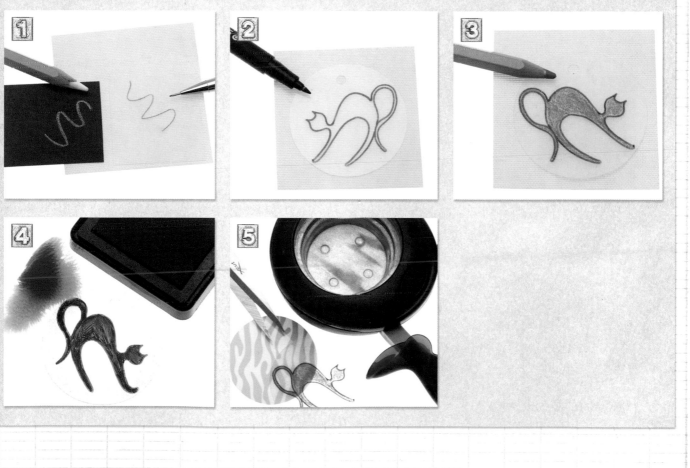

candy

Customize these cute charms to make a perfect pair of feline friends.

Everything you will need...

There are lots of sweet charms available, but sometimes they are not quite the finish you want. Follow these easy steps to make pretty earrings in the shade of your choice.

1 2 x metal cat charms

2 2 x silver earwires

3 Emery paper

4 Metal paint (color of your choice)

Cocktail stick

Paintbrush

2 x chain-nose pliers

candy

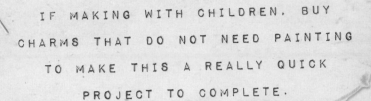

IF MAKING WITH CHILDREN, BUY
CHARMS THAT DO NOT NEED PAINTING
TO MAKE THIS A REALLY QUICK
PROJECT TO COMPLETE.

Assembling candy

1 When making earrings, it's best to make both at the same time to be sure they match. Take a small square of emery paper and lightly sand the cat charms.

2 Give the paint bottle a good shake or open and mix with a cocktail stick.

3 Paint in light strokes over the cat charm, holding the top loop with a pair of chain-nose pliers. Paint one side first, then set aside to dry. Paint the second side and leave to dry before painting the loop. If you paint in that order you can hold onto the body of the cat as you paint the top loop.

4 Take an earwire and open the loop (see page 22).

5 Place the cat charm on the earwire. Close the earwire by reversing the action you took to open it.

REMEMBER TO HAVE
THE CATS FACING IN
OPPOSITE DIRECTIONS
TO ACHIEVE A
MATCHING PAIR.

IF YOUR CAT CHARMS HAVE A HOLE FOR HANGING RATHER THAN A LOOP
AT THE TOP. JUST ADD TWO JUMPRINGS AND ATTACH THE CHARMS TO
THE EARWIRES WITH THE JUMPRINGS.

jinx

These tiny cat charms hanging from chains
give these delicate earrings a fun twist.

Everything you will need...

You'll need to use a fine chain for this project so that the balance between the charms and the chain is right. It will also help make sure the earrings are not too heavy to wear.

1 4 x bronze-colored cat charms (2 x 2 different styles)

2 2 x 2in (50mm) lengths of bronze-colored fine curb chain

3 6 x 5mm bronze-colored jumprings

4 2 x bronze-colored half-ball post with loop earrings

2 x chain-nose pliers

Assembling jinx

1 Open a jumpring (see page 22) and thread it through a link on the chain about a third of the way along. Keep the ring open.

2 Take one of the earrings and attach the jumpring from step 1 to the loop under the half ball. Close the jumpring.

3 Open another jumpring and attach it to one of the charms. Keep the ring open.

4 Add the charm with the jumpring open to the end of one of the chain lengths from step 2. Close the ring.

5 Open another jumpring and attach it to a cat charm (if you're using charms in different designs, add the second design here). Leave the jumpring open.

6 Attach the charm from step 5 to the end of the chain that doesn't have a charm already attached to complete the earring. Repeat these steps to make the second earring.

SMALL CAT CHARMS COME IN A WIDE VARIETY OF DESIGNS. LOOK FOR ONES THAT HAVE DIFFERENT STYLES BUT MATCH IN COLOR AND SIZE.

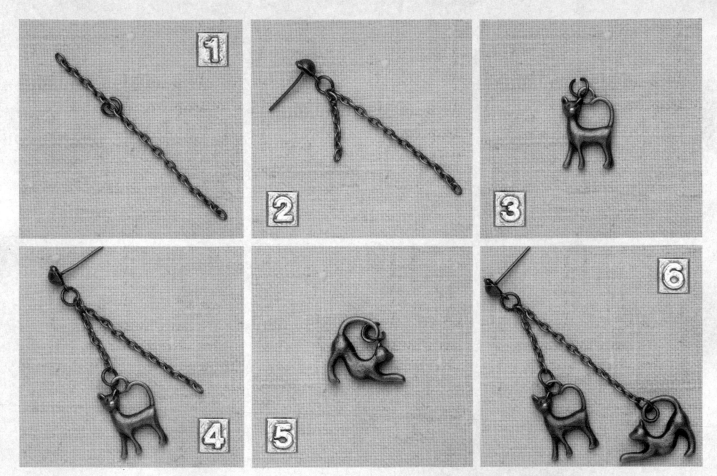

IF POSSIBLE TRY TO MATCH YOUR EARRINGS; HAVE
THEM MIRROR EACH OTHER BY HAVING THE CHARMS
FACING INWARD OR OUTWARD. SOME CHARMS—SUCH
AS THE STANDING CAT IN THIS PROJECT—DON'T ALLOW
THIS AS THEY HAVE A DEFINITE FRONT AND BACK.

samba

Take your inspiration
from a big cat and
go wild with these
leopard-print earrings!

Everything you will need...

All you need to make your own leopard-print beads
is a permanent marker pen and a little patience.

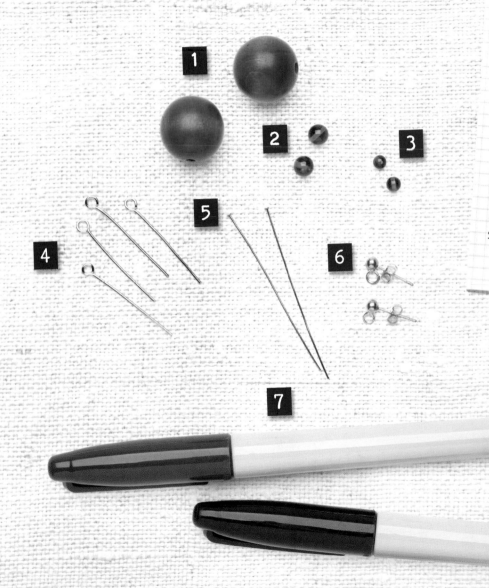

1. 2 x 18mm orange wooden beads
2. 2 x 6mm amber beads
3. 2 x 4mm amber beads
4. 4 x 2in (50mm) gold-colored eyepins
5. 2 x 2in (50mm) gold-colored headpins
6. 2 x gold-colored ball post with loop earrings
7. Black and brown permanent marker pens

Round-nose pliers

Chain-nose pliers

Side cutters

Assembling samba

1 Take the black marker pen and a wooden bead; draw small, squiggly semicircles all over the bead with a small dot in the center of each circle. If you look at leopard spots, they are circular but don't make completely enclosed shapes. Be careful to keep the shapes even so that you end up with a regular pattern all the way around the bead.

2 Take the brown marker pen and draw in the middle of the circles, as shown.

3 Take an eyepin and thread on a 6mm amber bead. Make a simple loop at the open end (see page 24), then take a leopard-print bead and attach to an eyepin in the same way.

4 Take a headpin and thread on a 4mm amber bead. Make a simple loop at the open end.

5 Take one of the 6mm beads and open one loop; attach this to the leopard-print bead and close the loop.

6 Open the free loop on the leopard-print bead and add the 4mm bead on the headpin.

7 Open the free loop on the 6mm bead and attach to the loop on the earring piece. Repeat the steps to make a matching pair of earrings.

PRACTISE THE LEOPARD-
PRINT PATTERN ON PAPER
BEFORE YOU START ON THE
BEAD. THE MARKER IS
PERMANENT SO YOU WON'T
BE ABLE TO CORRECT IT.

paddy

These tiny paw prints
are as cute as a kitten!

Everything you will need...

These little stud earrings are about $^3/_8$ in (9mm),
which makes them perfect to wear all day, every day!
And all you need to make them is a tiny scrap of clay.

1 Metallic copper polymer clay

2 2 x $^1/_4$in (6mm) flat pad posts (with scroll backs)

3 Craft knife

4 2 x 2in (50mm) squares of Teflon sheet

5 E6000 glue

2 x chain-nose pliers

Assembling paddy

1 Take a pea-size piece of clay and roll it into a log shape about $1/8$in (2mm) wide.

2 With the craft knife cut eight equal-size pieces from the roll about $1/16$in (1.5mm) long. The exact size doesn't matter too much so long as all the pieces are about the same size.

3 Take another piece of clay and make two identical balls about $3/16$in (5mm) big. Roll them, individually, into balls. Also roll the tiny slivers from step 2 into balls.

4 Place the larger ball on a piece of Teflon sheet and arrange four of the smaller balls in a line on one side; it should look like a paw at this point. Repeat with the other larger ball and the remaining four smaller balls on the other piece of Teflon sheet. This stage is done on the Teflon so you can transfer the paws into the oven without needing to pick them up as they are very delicate.

5 Make sure your Teflon sheets with the paws in place are on a firm surface, then press gently on the paws with your forefinger. Use a firm pressure so that all the balls squash together and stick. Don't wiggle your finger around, just press straight down.

6 Bake the paw shapes in a toaster oven or a standard oven at the temperature recommended by the clay manufacturer (this will differ depending on the brand of clay you have). Once baked, let the paws cool, and then they will come straight off the sheet. Using a tiny dot of E6000 glue, attach the earstud pads to the backs of the paws.

SOMETIMES THE PAWS COME APART AFTER FIRING, SO IT IS A GOOD IDEA TO MAKE MORE THAN TWO AT THE SAME TIME. THEN YOU ARE GUARANTEED TO HAVE AT LEAST TWO THAT MATCH AND HAVE STUCK TOGETHER.

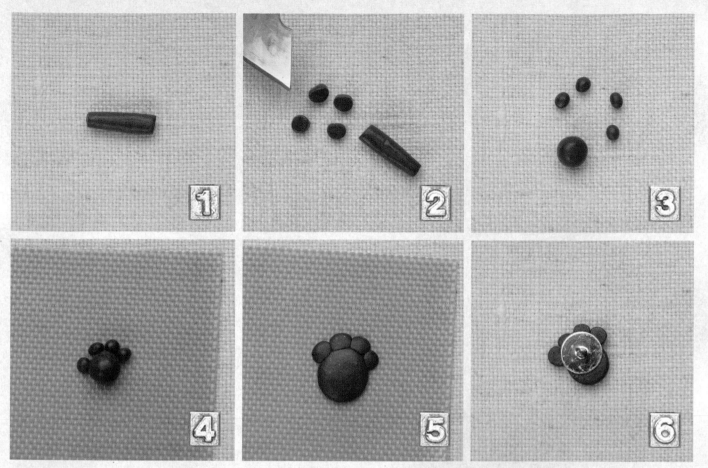

YOU CAN MAKE THESE PAWS AT WHATEVER SIZE YOU WISH. BUT AS YOU GO BIGGER YOU WILL NEED SOMETHING FLAT TO PRESS THEM WITH AS YOUR FINGER WON'T BE LARGE ENOUGH.

COCO

Be cool as a cat with this
quirky silhouette pendant.

Everything you will need...

Shrink plastic is easy and fun to work with, so any silhouette with a clear outline will work for this pendant. This stretching cat is an elegant choice.

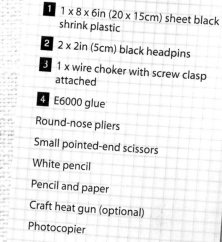

1. 1 x 8 x 6in (20 x 15cm) sheet black shrink plastic
2. 2 x 2in (5cm) black headpins
3. 1 x wire choker with screw clasp attached
4. E6000 glue

Round-nose pliers

Small pointed-end scissors

White pencil

Pencil and paper

Craft heat gun (optional)

Photocopier

SHRINK PLASTIC COMES IN A VARIETY OF COLORS. THIS PENDANT WOULD LOOK GREAT IN ANY COLOR.

Assembling coco

1 Photocopy the template below at 200%. Cut the paper shape out with the scissors.

2 Using a white pencil, trace around the shape on the matte side of the shrink plastic.

3 Cut the shape out carefully using the pointed-end scissors. Shrink plastic can tear so be gentle when cutting out. When you get to the bit in between the tail and body, pierce through the center of the space with the scissors and cut out toward the line, then follow the line around.

4 Shrink the shape with a craft heat gun or in a toaster or electric oven at around 275–300°F (135–150°C); see page 26 for tips. For a complicated shape like this cat, the heat gun works better than an oven as you can control the shrinking more easily.

5 Take the black headpins and round-nose pliers. Hold the head end of the headpin in-between the pliers about halfway along the jaws and wind around once to make a complete loop. Check the loop fits over the clasp on the wire choker before continuing. If it does not fit, then gently widen the loop by pushing it down the plier jaw a little more, then continue to coil the whole headpin. Coil toward the plier handles so the coil doesn't taper with the plier jaws. Make two.

6 Choose which side of the cat you want to be the front—one side is matte, the other shiny—and glue the coils on the back side in the middle of the cat's back, keeping the coils level. Leave to dry completely.

7 Unscrew the wire choker and thread the cat on to finish the necklace.

SOLID SHAPES SHRINK BETTER, SO IF YOU ARE STRUGGLING WITH THE CAT'S LEGS AND TAIL, TRY A DIFFERENT-SHAPED CAT. THERE ARE LOTS OF IMAGES AVAILABLE ONLINE.

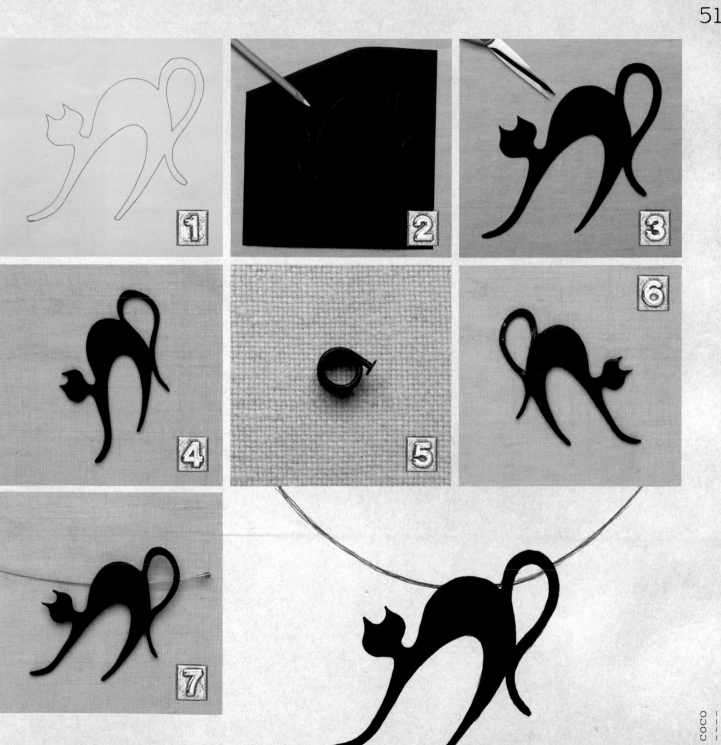

gracie

A gorgeous glass cat
bead is the focal point
of this necklace.

Everything you will need...

I found this delightful glass cat on the Internet; it was handmade by a lampwork-glass artist. Have fun sourcing one for your necklace, as there are many artists around the world making beautiful glass pieces.

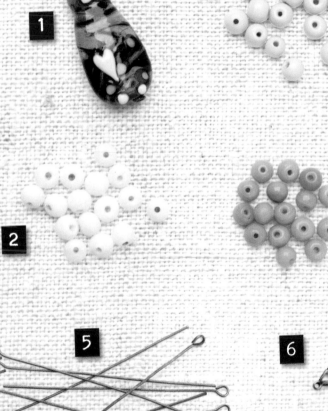

1 1 x lampwork-glass cat bead (hole running top to bottom)

2 16 x 6mm white glass beads

3 16 x 6mm blue glass beads

4 16 x 6mm brown glass beads

5 49 x 2in (50mm) antique bronze-colored eyepins

6 1 x antique bronze-colored trigger clasp

7 1 x 5mm antique bronze-colored jumpring

2 x chain-nose pliers

Round-nose pliers

Side cutters

Assembling gracie

1 Take an eyepin and, using a pair of chain-nose pliers, grasp across the eye on the pin and bend to a right angle as close to the eye as possible.

2 Thread the cat bead onto the eyepin and create a wrapped loop at the top (see page 25). You will need to work slowly and gently, as the glass bead can break easily. Lay to one side.

3 Take the other 48 eyepins and thread one 6mm bead onto each pin. Make a simple loop at the open end on each one (see page 24).

4 Take one of the blue beads from step 3 and open the loop (see page 22). Thread on one of the brown beads and then close the loop. Open the opposite loop on the brown bead and attach a white one. Repeat this step until you have a chain with eight beads of each color attached (that's 24 beads in total). Make a second chain in exactly the same way so you have two matching chains.

5 Take one of the chains and open the end loop of a blue bead. Thread on the glass cat from step 2. Close the loop and open the end loop of the other chain and attach that to the cat. Close the loop.

6 To finish the necklace, open the loop at the free end of the chain and attach the clasp, then close the loop. Open the loop on the end of the other chain, add the 5mm jumpring, and close the loop.

I MATCHED THE COLOR OF THE 6MM BEADS TO THE LAMPWORK CAT, SO BUY THE CAT BEAD FIRST AND THEN MATCH YOUR 6MM BEADS TO IT.

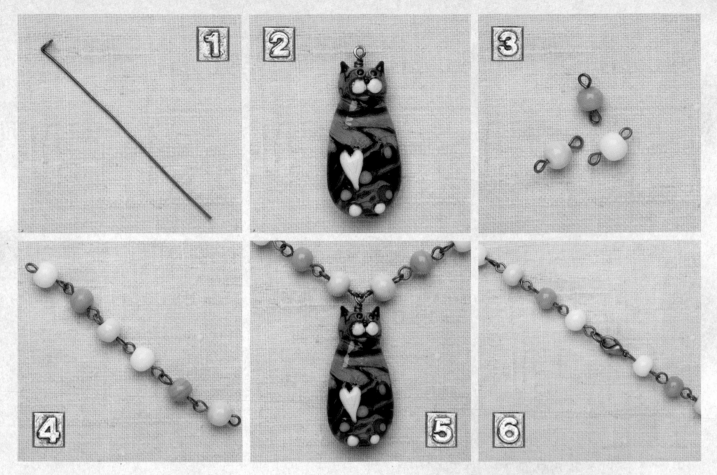

IF YOU WANT TO GIVE EXTRA PROTECTION
TO THE DELICATE GLASS BEAD ADD A SMALLER
BEAD TO THE EYEPIN SO THE WRAPPED LOOP
IS FARTHER AWAY FROM THE CAT.

gracie

polly

Keep your beloved pet
always close by with this
lovely portrait necklace.

Everything you will need...

Pendant blanks and glass cabochons make creating a personalized pendant really easy.

1 1 x 1in (25mm) square silver-colored pendant blank

2 1 x 1in (25mm) square glass cabochon

3 Cat picture

4 Finished necklace chain

PVA glue

Glue brush

Cyanoacrylate glue

Small sharp scissors

Pencil

Ruler

Sticky tack

Assembling polly

1 Print a photo of the cat; you'll need the image to be at least 1in (25mm) in size. Use the glass cabochon to select the part of the image you want to feature in the pendant.

2 Hold the cabochon in place and mark all four sides with a pencil. Don't draw all the way around as the cabochon's corners are slightly rounded and you need a sharp square edge.

3 Take the ruler and line it up with your marks from step 2, then draw in the complete lines so they cross over in the corners. Cut the shape out with sharp-pointed scissors.

4 Take the PVA glue and coat the picture. Make sure you coat both sides and go right over the edges. Do this in two steps, allowing the first side to dry before turning over to coat the other side. This will stop the cyanoacrylate glue from soaking into the paper and spoiling the pendant.

5 When you are sure the picture is completely dry, place a small drop of cyanoacrylate glue in the pendant and place the picture over the top. Smooth over the picture to make sure the glue spreads out. Allow to completely dry.

6 Place another couple of drops of cyanoacrylate glue on the picture and place the glass cabochon on top. With a piece of sticky tack, push down firmly on the glass cabochon—this will force any air bubbles out from under the glass and will also spread the glue out to an even, thin coat. Hold until you are sure the glue will stay in place, then leave the tack on the glass until the pendant has completely dried.

7 Take the tack off the glass and thread the chain through the pendant bail to finish.

BE CAREFUL NOT TO USE TOO MUCH CYANOACRYLATE GLUE, BECAUSE IT IS THIN IT WILL SPREAD A LONG WAY AND COULD STICK YOU TO THE PENDANT TOO!

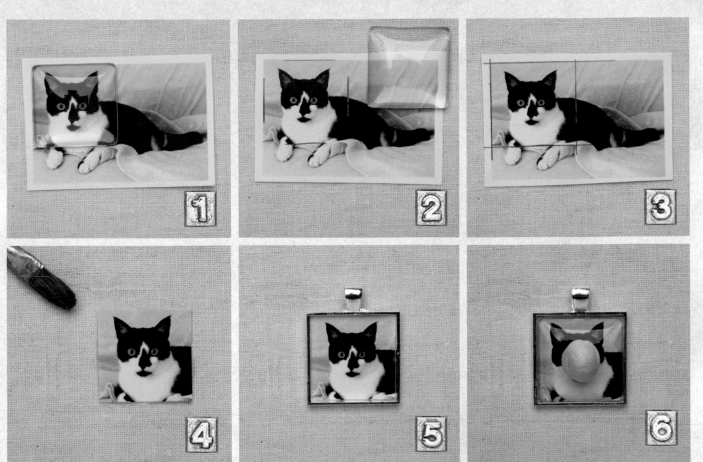

PENDANT BLANKS COME IN LOTS OF
DIFFERENT SHAPES AND FINISHES SO PICK
THE STYLE THAT SUITS YOU THE BEST.
YOU COULD ATTACH IT TO A KEYRING
IF YOU PREFER.

oscar

Go monochrome with
this elegant white
tiger beaded necklace.

Everything you will need...

This necklace uses a simple combination of tiny black and white seed beads with a tiger bead with the hole running top to bottom.

1 1 x 1¼ x ¾in (30 x 18mm) tiger bead (with vertical hole)

2 ½ oz (15g) x 1.8mm (size 11) shiny white seed beads

3 ½ oz (15g) x 1.8mm (size 11) matte black seed beads

4 Black and white beading thread

2 x beading needles

Scissors

Beading mat

1

3

2

4

Assembling oscar

1 Measure the length for your necklace by winding the black thread around your neck and down to your waist. Double the length and cut it off at your waist. This will give you a long enough piece to make the necklace with a little to spare for knotting the ends. Thread onto a beading needle.

2 Holding both ends of the thread together, make a knot in the end. Pull the needle to the center of the thread (making a double thread), pull the knot tight and cut off the thread end as close to the knot as possible. Place a pile of black seed beads on your work surface (a beading mat is useful here) and start by stringing a single bead onto the thread. Bring the needle around the bead and in between the two threads to secure the bead. Continue threading beads to make a 3-in (75-mm) length of black seed beads.

3 Measure the white thread as in step 1 and thread onto a beading needle. Repeat step 2 with the white beads.

4 Take both beading needles with the 3in (75mm) of seed beads threaded on and thread on the tiger bead from the bottom so that the threads come out of the tiger's back and the beaded thread sits under the tiger's belly.

5 You need to make sure that the necklace will be long enough for your head to fit through the beaded strands without the need for a clasp. To do this, place the tiger bead and the white thread on your work surface and take up the black thread. String on enough seed beads to allow your head to fit through the gap, take the needle through the tiger bead and try it over your head to check if it's long enough, being very careful of the needles. After trying on the necklace, pull the needle back out of the tiger bead and keep adding beads until you are happy with the length.

6 As soon as the black beaded chain is the right length, lay it down on your work surface and repeat step 5 with the white beads. You will not need to try it on again as you can use the black strand as the guide for the white; both strands should be exactly the same length. When you have both strands the same length take both needles through the tiger bead.

7 Under the tiger bead, add enough seed beads to each thread to make them equal to the ones already done in step 2. To secure the ends, bring the thread around the outside of the final bead and thread up through a couple of beads. Make a knot by wrapping the thread attached to the needle around the back of the thread running through the beads, bring the needle across the front of the thread, and push it through the loop it creates and pull tight (this is called a half-hitch knot). Repeat this a couple of times to secure the thread and cut off the excess.

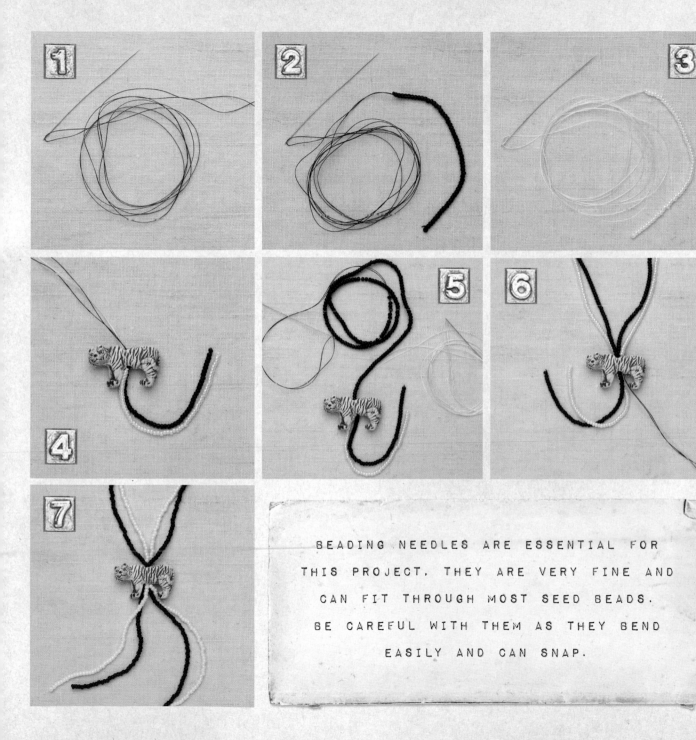

BEADING NEEDLES ARE ESSENTIAL FOR
THIS PROJECT. THEY ARE VERY FINE AND
CAN FIT THROUGH MOST SEED BEADS.
BE CAREFUL WITH THEM AS THEY BEND
EASILY AND CAN SNAP.

bracelets & rings

luna

This pretty patterned
cat button makes a
colorful ring.

Everything you will need...

Decoupage is a great way to decorate anything, so when I saw these lovely cat buttons, they just shouted out to be patterned.

1 1 x cat-shaped plastic button

2 1 x ring with $3/8$in (9mm) flat pad

3 Small piece of patterned paper

4 2in (50mm) square of emery paper

5 Decoupage glue

6 Polyurethane gloss varnish

Glue brush

E6000 glue

Container for glue

Small sharp scissors

Pencil

Craft knife

Cutting mat

USE THIS SAME TECHNIQUE TO MAKE EARSTUDS BY GLUING THE DECOUPAGE CAT TO A STUD WITH A FLAT PAD.

luna

Assembling luna

1 Take the button and sand the front to provide a key for the decoupage.

2 With the patterned paper and a pencil, draw an outline of the cat button on the back of the paper. Take your time to work out which part of the paper pattern you want on the cat.

3 Cut out the cat shape leaving $\frac{1}{8}$in (3mm) around the outside of the pencil line. After cutting the shape out, go around the edge and make small cuts up to the pencil line to make the edge into lots of little tabs. This helps the paper bend around the shape when you glue it on.

4 Pour a small amount of decoupage glue into a container and paint a layer of glue on the front of the cat button. Holding the button by the shank on the back, carefully place the paper on the cat, lining up the pencil outline to the edge of the cat. Paint a layer of glue over the top of the paper.

5 With a tiny amount of glue on your brush, go around the edge and paste each tab down the sides. Work slowly and make sure you take off any spare glue with the brush as you go. Leave the button to dry completely.

6 Take the craft knife and carefully cut the shank off the back of the button. As it's plastic it should be fairly easy to cut off, but this should only be done by an adult.

7 Take the ring blank and sand the flat pad, then place a small amount of glue on the pad and stick the cat button down. Leave to completely dry before wearing.

IF THE BUTTON IS MADE OF SOFT PLASTIC, YOU CAN CUT OFF THE SHANK WITH AN OLD PAIR OF SIDE CUTTERS. DON'T USE A NEW PAIR AS IT COULD BLUNT THEM.

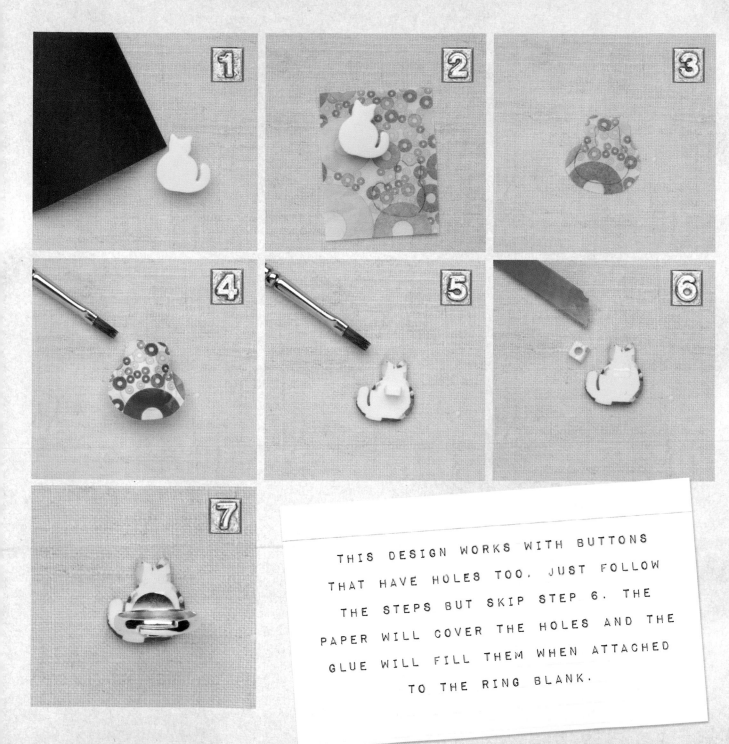

THIS DESIGN WORKS WITH BUTTONS
THAT HAVE HOLES TOO. JUST FOLLOW
THE STEPS BUT SKIP STEP 6. THE
PAPER WILL COVER THE HOLES AND THE
GLUE WILL FILL THEM WHEN ATTACHED
TO THE RING BLANK.

molly

Cat ears turn this simple wire
ring into something extra special.

Everything you will need...

Wire alone can make the best jewelry; simply take
two gauges of wire and create a cute, quirky ring.

1 10in (250mm) of US 20 gauge
(SWG 21, 0.8mm) copper wire

2 10in (250mm) of US 26 gauge
(SWG 27, 0.4mm) copper wire

3 Ring mandrel

4 Glue

Masking tape

Chain-nose pliers

Side cutters

18 GAUGE (SWG 19, 1MM) WIRE WOULD WORK BUT IT WILL BE HARDER TO FORM INTO THE INITIAL SHAPE AS THICKER WIRE IS STIFFER TO START WITH.

Assembling molly

1 Take the 20 gauge wire and find the center; it doesn't have to be exact. Hold the wire in chain-nose pliers about halfway down the jaws and bend the wire up each side of the jaws in the same direction to make a square "U" shape.

2 Move the pliers so the jaws are gripping one side of the "U", holding the wire right at the handle end in the jaws. Bend the wire end to a right angle against the pliers. Repeat for the other side.

3 Again move the pliers to the end of the wire, holding against the bend you made in step 2. Hold the wire in the jaws up at the handle end and bend the wire against the pliers so you make what looks like a step. Look at the photo here to check you are bending the wire in the right direction. Repeat for the other side.

4 Looking at the wire, you should have six bends. Counting from the left, hold the wire in the point of the chain-nose pliers next to bend two and push it past the right angle to make a triangle shape (like a cat's ear). Now count to bend five and do the same. This should have pushed the outside wire to sit in line with the wire in-between the ears.

5 Take a small strip of masking tape and tape the wire piece to the ring mandrel, in-between the ears. This will keep the wire steady as you bend it around the mandrel.

6 Bend the wire ends once each side around the mandrel and back to the opposite side to the ears on the mandrel, then twist the wires together a couple of times. This is just to hold the wire in place so don't worry if it doesn't look neat.

7 Take the ring off the mandrel and check you are happy with the shape.

8 Take the piece of 26 gauge wire and, starting on the outside of one ear, wrap the wire around the ring shank four times on the outside of the ear. Then take the 26 gauge wire through the ear and continue to wrap it along the ring. Keep wrapping in between the ears and inside the second ear, then finally wrap four times on the outside of the second ear. Use the side cutters to cut off any excess wire, making sure the cut is on the outside of the ring so it doesn't catch on the skin.

9 Untwist the wires on the ring shank and snip these ends off flat against where the 26 gauge wire wrapping starts. Add a tiny drop of glue to the very ends to hold the wires in place.

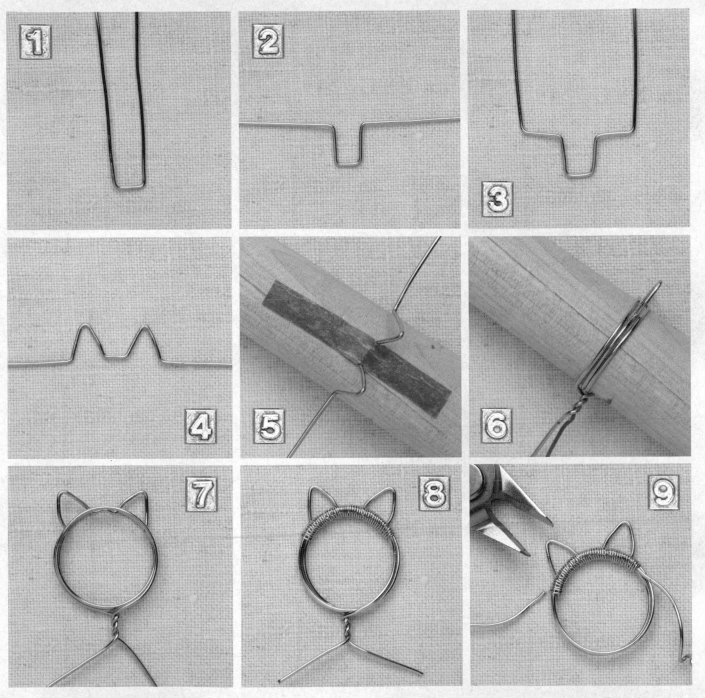

kitty

Adorn your wrist and make
a statement with a colorful
leather bracelet and cat charms.

Everything you will need...

Team brightly coloured leather with cool cat charms to make the perfect bracelet for a trendsetter.

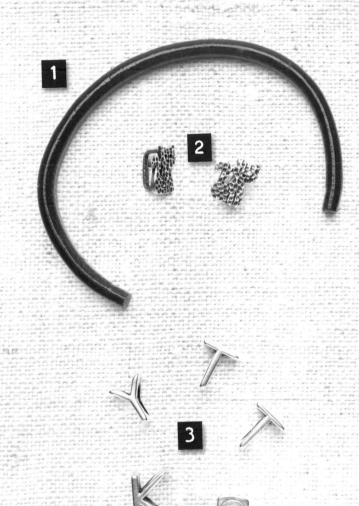

1 1 x ³⁄₈in (10mm) colored licorice leather

2 2 x licorice leather cat charm

3 5 x licorice leather alphabet charms

4 1 x licorice leather magnetic clasp

Craft knife

Glue

Measuring tape

Marker pen

Cutting mat

kitty

Assembling kitty

1 Measure your wrist, allowing a bit of room for movement. Remember that the clasp will add ¹/₂in (12mm) to the size.

2 Carefully cut the leather to your required length. Do this on a cutting mat using a craft knife.

3 Take one end of the clasp and place a small amount of glue in the end. Push the leather in as far as it will go. Leave to dry.

4 When the glue has dried, thread on the charms in the order you want them.

5 Take the piece of the clasp that has not been used and place a small amount of glue in the end. As in step 3, push onto the end of the leather as far as you can. Leave to dry.

6 Finally, move the charms around until you are happy with where they sit, then place a tiny dot of glue on the inside to hold each charm in place.

LICORICE LEATHER VARIES SLIGHTLY IN SIZE SO MAKE SURE YOUR CHARMS MATCH THE SIZE OF THE LEATHER. IF POSSIBLE BUY ALL THE COMPONENTS FROM THE SAME SUPPLIER.

ALPHABET CHARMS ARE GREAT; YOU CAN
SPELL OUT ANY WORD OR NAME. IT COULD
BE THE NAME OF YOUR PET OR A PERSON.

milo

Large leopard-print
coins make this chic
bracelet stand out.

Everything you will need...

Realize the wild cat in you! Make a stunning bracelet using printed coin beads and some elegant seed beads.

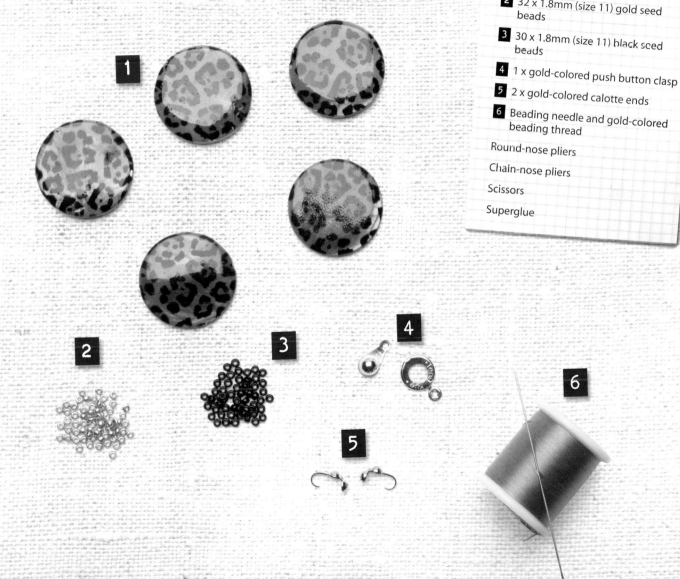

1. 5 x 25mm leopard-print coin beads
2. 32 x 1.8mm (size 11) gold seed beads
3. 30 x 1.8mm (size 11) black seed beads
4. 1 x gold-colored push button clasp
5. 2 x gold-colored calotte ends
6. Beading needle and gold-colored beading thread

Round-nose pliers

Chain-nose pliers

Scissors

Superglue

milo

Assembling milo

1 Take a calotte end; use a pair of round-nose pliers to curl the hook end around until it meets itself to make a loop. Open it slightly, attach one end of the button clasp, and close the loop again.

2 Thread the needle with a long length of thread and double it up. Knot the end of the thread and then add on a gold seed bead. Take the needle back through in between the two threads between the bead and the knot. Pull tight to secure the bead.

3 Pick up the calotte and clasp piece from step 1 and feed the needle through the calotte from the inside. Pull the thread until the seed bead is sitting inside the calotte cup.

4 Take three black and two gold seed beads and thread them alternately on to the needle. Next add a leopard-print bead, then another three black and two gold seed beads. Continue to do this until you have threaded all five leopard print beads and finish with a row of seed beads.

5 Take the remaining calotte and thread it on from the outside of the cup. Now thread on a gold seed bead and bring the thread around the bead and back through the hole in the calotte. Pull until the calotte sits tightly up against the row of seed beads on the outside.

6 Start the second row of seed beads with three gold and two black beads, alternating as in step 4. Add a row and thread the needle back through the leopard-print bead. Add another three gold and two black seed beads through the next leopard-print bead. Repeat this until you reach the end.

7 At the end, thread the needle through the hole in the calotte from the outside. Thread on a seed bead to sit inside the cup. Take the needle through the seed bead a couple of times to secure and add a tiny drop of superglue to hold it in place. Let the glue dry, then cut off the excess thread. Attach the loop section of the button clasp to the calotte as in step 1.

8 Using a pair of chain-nose pliers, gently close the calotte cup by placing the cups in the jaws of the pliers and squeezing.

9 Go back to the calotte at the opposite end of the bracelet and close the calotte in the same way as in step 8.

TO SIMPLIFY THIS BRACELET REMOVE THE SEED BEADS AND ADD 8MM BEADS IN BETWEEN THE LEOPARD-PRINT COINS ALL THREADED ONTO ELASTICATED BEADING THREAD.

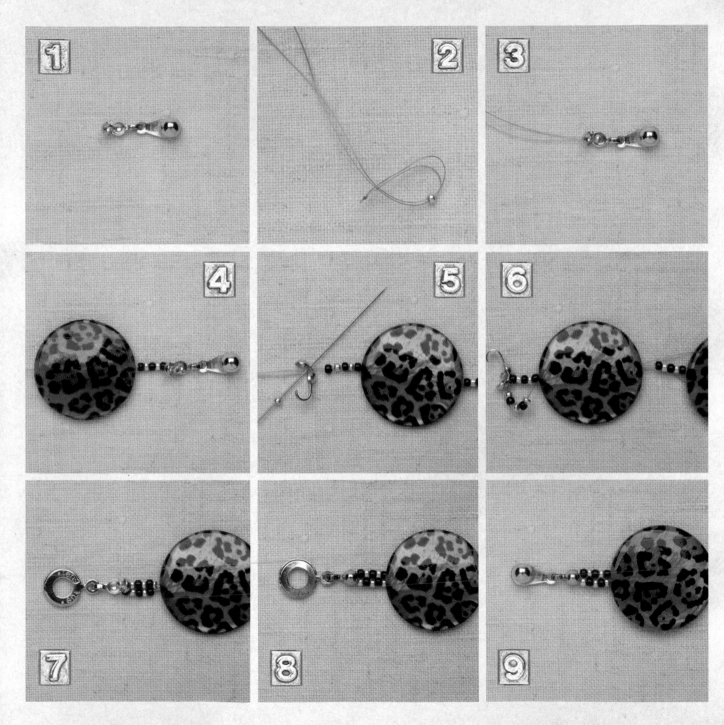

brooches &
cuff links

trigger

Add some character to
your cuffs with these
crafty cats.

Everything you will need...

Simple yet very effective, fun cat- and mouse-shaped buttons make great novelty cuff links.

1. 2 x cat-shape buttons with shanks
2. 2 x mouse-shape buttons with shanks
3. Gold paint
4. 8 x 5mm brass-colored jumprings
5. Small paintbrush

2 x chain-nose pliers

trigger

IF YOU REQUIRE
A LONGER SECTION
BETWEEN THE BUTTONS
THEN ADD IN EXTRA
JUMPRINGS.

Assembling trigger

1 Take the cat and mouse buttons and coat with the gold paint. Leave to dry.

2 Take the mouse buttons and attach a jumpring (see page 24) to the shank on the back of each one, then close the jumprings.

3 Take another jumpring and attach to the backs of each cat button. Close the jumprings.

4 Attach a second jumpring to the first one on each of the cat buttons and close the jumprings.

5 Attach a second jumpring to each of the closed jumprings on the mouse buttons. Leave these jumprings open.

6 Take the cats and add to the open jumprings on the mouse button. Close the jumprings to finish.

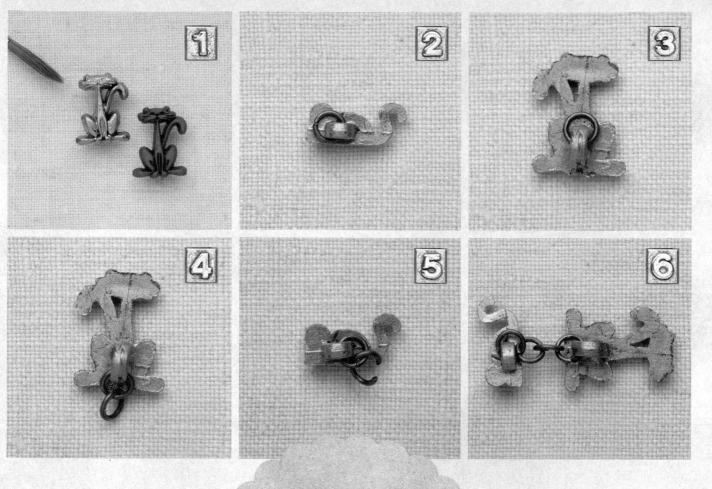

YOU COULD HAVE THE
CAT BUTTONS BACK TO
BACK AS ONE CUFF
LINK AND THE TWO
MICE TOGETHER ON
THE OTHER SLEEVE
IF YOU WISH.

felix

Cute and colorful paw prints are ideal adornments for a pair of cuff links.

Everything you will need...

Polymer clay is a great material for this kind of project as you can bake one part, then add unbaked clay and bake the whole thing again! This keeps the color separation sharp and stops the paw print from going out of shape.

1. 1in (25mm) square by $\frac{1}{2}$in (12mm) thick block of blue polymer clay
2. $\frac{1}{2}$in (12mm) ball of pearl white clay
3. 2 x silver-colored cuff links with $\frac{3}{8}$in (10mm) pad
4. E6000 glue
5. Polyurethane gloss varnish

$\frac{13}{16}$ x $\frac{1}{2}$in (20 x 12mm) oval cutter

$\frac{3}{8}$in (10mm) round cutter

$\frac{1}{8}$in (2mm) round cutter

2in (50mm) square of emery paper

Paintbrush

Teflon sheet

Roller

Spacers or playing cards

Sticky tack

Assembling felix

1 Working on a Teflon sheet, condition the polymer clay by flattening it out with a roller, folding it over and repeating until soft. Then roll it out to about $1/16$ in (1.5mm) thick using the spacers. If you're using playing cards you will need a stack of four each side of the clay. You will need a large enough sheet to cut out four ovals. Using the oval cutter, cut out two ovals but don't remove them from the surrounding clay yet as the clay works to protect the shapes from distorting.

2 With the $3/8$ in (10mm) and $1/8$ in (2mm) round cutters (using the step photo as reference), cut out a paw shape. The $3/8$ in cutter will make the pad of the paw and the $1/8$ in one makes the four toes. Try to stop the clay coming out with the cutter as it's still protecting the shape from distorting.

3 When all the pieces are cut out, gently remove all the cutout pieces to reveal the paw shape.

4 Place the piece from step 3 back on top of the rolled out blue sheet of clay from step 1.

5 Take the oval cutter and, lining it up with the oval shape, press down to cut through the bottom sheet too. As you push down, the two sheets will press together. Bake the pieces following the clay manufacturer's directions

6 When the baked clay pieces have cooled, fill in the cutout paw shapes with the pearl white clay, pressing the clay into the holes to make sure there are no air holes. Allow the white clay to be slightly higher than the blue and don't worry if it looks a little messy. Bake again to the same temperature.

7 When the clay has cooled again, sand the fronts until the paw outlines look clean and sharp.

8 Sand the cuff link pad and glue the polymer paw prints to the cuff link. Leave to dry.

9 Stand the cuff links up with a little sticky tack and paint the whole polymer piece with a coat of gloss varnish. Leave to dry before wearing.

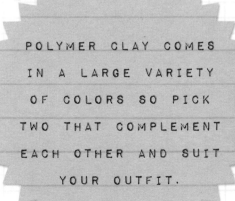

POLYMER CLAY COMES IN A LARGE VARIETY OF COLORS SO PICK TWO THAT COMPLEMENT EACH OTHER AND SUIT YOUR OUTFIT.

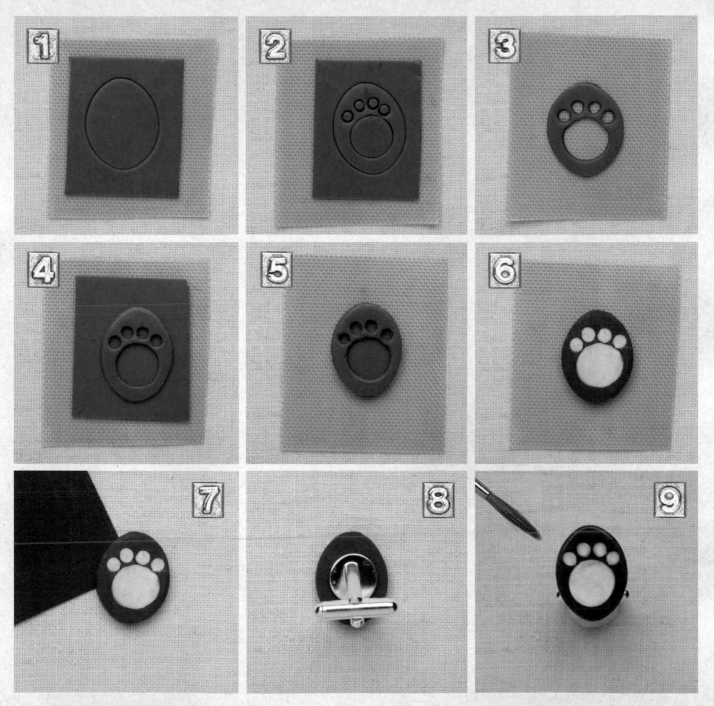

leo

Wear a lion with pride
on this fabulous brooch!

Everything you will need...

Shrink plastic is one of the best materials currently available to play with—it's so versatile and great fun for kids. Make any big cat fan happy with this lion-head brooch.

1 1 x 8½ x 11in (A4) sheet of frosted shrink plastic

2 Colored pencils: dark brown, terracotta, yellow, white, and golden brown

3 Fine-tip black permanent marker

4 Polyurethane matte varnish

5 1 x 1in (25mm) brooch pin

Small sharp scissors

E6000 glue

Paintbrush

Craft heat gun (optional)

Assembling leo

1 Photocopy the template provided at 200% and lay the shrink plastic sheet over the top, shiny side up. Trace the outline of the lion's face on the shrink plastic using permanent marker. The marker must be the permanent type or the ink will smudge. Make sure you fill in the nose with the marker.

2 Turn the plastic over and start by coloring in the lion's face using the white pencil for the lower jaw, the muzzle, and the eye. Then use the golden-brown pencil for the rest of the face and ear.

3 Now color in the rest of the mane using the yellow for the piece around the ear, then the terracotta for the next section, and the dark brown for the outer mane.

4 When the whole image is colored in, cut around the edge with the scissors, being careful to cut just outside the black line.

5 Shrink the lion face with a craft heat gun or in a toaster or electric oven at around 275–300°F (135–150°C); see page 26 for tips.

6 When the lion has cooled, seal the back with a layer of matte varnish. This will stop the pencil from staining clothes. Let the varnish dry completely then stick the brooch pin on with E6000 glue.

FIND PICTURES OF ANIMALS IN BOOKS OR ONLINE AND COPY THE OUTLINES. LET CHILDREN COLOR IN THE PICTURES AND THEN SEE THEIR WONDER AS THE IMAGES SHRINK IN THE OVEN.

THIS BROOCH COULD ALSO BE MADE INTO A KEYRING BY PUNCHING OUT A HOLE AT THE TOP OF THE HEAD BEFORE SHRINKING. YOU CAN USE A STANDARD OFFICE HOLE PUNCH AS THE PLASTIC IS SO THIN.

avalon

A picture of a vintage
cat painting makes
a gorgeous brooch.

Everything you will need...

There are many royalty-free images available online to use in projects. I downloaded this image and printed it to the size I needed to make this lovely, vintage-style brooch.

1 1 x cat image

2 1 x ³⁄₄ x 1in (18 x 25mm) vintage-style oval bezel brooch blank

3 PVA glue

4 Clear resin

5 Resin hardener

6 Pencil

7 Small brush

8 Plastic food bag or plastic file pocket

Scrap of paper

Scissors

Mixing cups and sticks

Scrap polymer clay

Assembling avalon

1 Choose a cat image and print out using a color printer so the height is 1in (25mm) and the width is a minimum of $3/4$ in (18mm). You can print using standard printer paper, but use your printer on its photo setting to get the best-quality image.

2 Make a template of the bezel blank by holding a piece of paper over the blank and rubbing with a pencil around the edge to show where the bezel edge is.

3 Cut the shape out, cutting just inside the pencil line. Check the template fits comfortably in the blank.

4 Place the template over the cat image and trace around with a pencil. Cut the shape out.

5 Check the cat image sits nicely in the blank.

6 This step is very important: if you don't coat the image completely, the resin will soak into the paper and ruin the image. This process should be done on a plastic surface, such as a clear plastic file pocket or a plastic food bag. Take the PVA glue and brush a coat over the image, let it dry and coat the back, let that side dry, then coat the front for a second time. When completely dry, cut off any leftover glue from around the edge.

7 Mix up the resin in a small plastic cup—you'll need two parts resin to one part of hardener. Resin can be purchased in small bottles with dropper tops to make it easy to work out the ratios. This pendant will need about 12 drops of resin and six drops of hardener. Mix the resin with a stick carefully so you don't get a lot of bubbles in it. Place the blank where it can rest overnight, using a piece of scrap polymer clay to prop it up to make sure the bezel is completely level. Place the glue-coated cat image in the bezel and pour the resin over the top. Work slowly and fill to the top of the bezel.

8 Take a clean plastic cup and cover the piece so that no dust lands in the resin as it dries. Leave to dry for at least 12 hours and gently touch the very edge to check the resin is hard before you wear the brooch.

IF YOU ARE NOT CONFIDENT IN MIXING RESIN LOOK FOR RESIN THAT DOESN'T NEED A HARDENER AS THERE ARE MANY BRANDS THAT WORK IN DIFFERENT WAYS.

YOU CAN USE AN OLD POSTCARD OR A PICTURE YOU ALREADY HAVE INSTEAD OF DOWNLOADING AN IMAGE FROM THE INTERNET.

hair
accessories

star

Turn a photo of your
favorite family pet
into a cool hair slide.

Everything you will need...

This technique of taking a laser-printed image and transferring it to polymer clay is simply amazing and quite easy!

1. Photo-quality laser-printed image
2. 1oz (28g) pearl-white polymer clay
3. 2½in (60mm) hair barrette
4. Tissue blade
5. Spacers (or playing cards)
6. E6000 glue

Scissors

Craft knife

Pencil

Ruler

Roller

Water

Heatproof gloves

Teflon sheet

star

Assembling star

1 Using appropriate computer software, create a good-quality version of the photograph you want and print it out slightly bigger than the hair slide on standard printer paper (not photo paper). **Note:** this process works only with laser-printed images; ink-jet will not work.

2 Using a pencil and ruler, mark the outline for the hair slide, making it approximately 1$\frac{1}{2}$in (38mm) high by 3in (75mm) long. Cut the shape out with scissors or a craft knife.

3 Working on a Teflon sheet, condition the polymer clay by flattening it out with a roller, folding it over and repeating until soft. Roll out the clay using the roller, with spacers (or a stack of four playing cards) either side of the clay. Roll until it is big enough to place the image on with a little extra space around the edge.

4 Place the image ink side down on the polymer clay and gently press to make sure there are no air bubbles between the clay and the paper. Leave it for about two minutes.

5 Dip your finger in a small cup of cold water and spread the water across the back of the image. Press the water into the paper gently. As you work, the picture will start to be revealed. Look carefully at the image and keep adding water until you are sure you can see the image clearly.

6 Give the water time to soak into the paper. Then, using your finger with more water, gently rub the paper away. Rub in circles, adding more water to keep the paper wet. Be very gentle! The paper will come off in layers and this process will take a while to get all the paper off.

7 As soon as the paper has gone the photo should be revealed as a reversed version of what you had printed. Don't touch the image, as it will be slightly sticky. Take the tissue blade and cut out the image, or use a craft knife and ruler.

8 Bake the clay at the manufacturer's recommended temperature. Take the piece out of the oven and, before it cools down, bend into a slight curve. Wear heatproof gloves to do this. It's not vital to make this bend, but the slide looks nice with a slight curve.

9 Stick the hair barrette to the back of the polymer piece, making it as central as possible with E6000 glue. Leave to completely dry before wearing.

IF USING AN IMAGE WITH WORDS MAKE SURE YOU REVERSE THE WORDS BEFORE YOU PRINT THE IMAGE OUT OR THEY WILL NOT BE READABLE ON THE FINISHED PIECE.

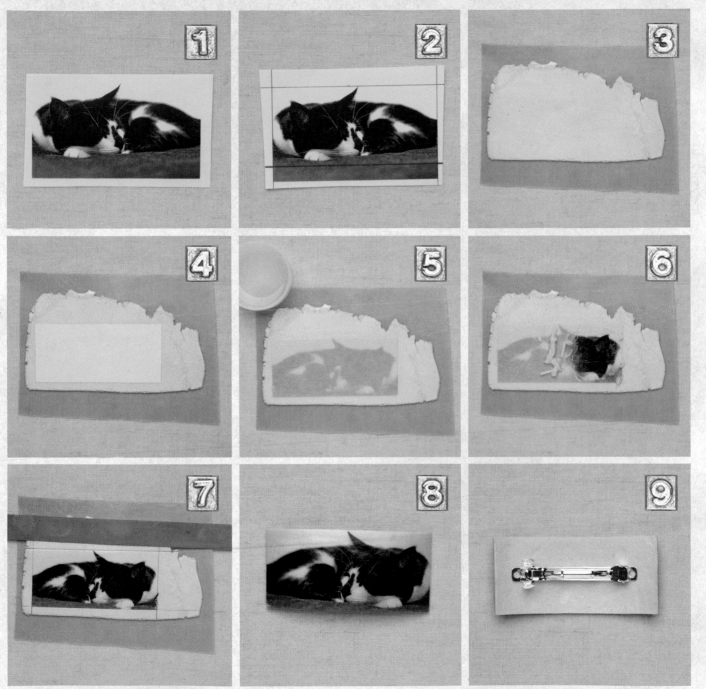

nala

Sparkle like a
kitten in these
purr-fect ears!

Everything you will need...

There is nothing better than a pair of sparkly crystal-bead cat ears to liven up any party outfit and cause a stir.

1 80 x 4mm bright orange crystal beads

2 1 x 13in (330mm) gold-colored headband

3 30in (89cm) x US 18 gauge (SWG 19, 1mm) gold-colored wire

4 39in (1m) x US 24 gauge (SWG 25, 0.5mm) gold-colored wire

Chain-nose pliers

Side cutters

Measuring tape

Marker pen

Assembling nala

1 Take the measuring tape and marker pen. Measure up from the end of the band 4$\frac{1}{2}$in (115mm) and make a mark on the band; repeat for the other side. From that mark, measure 2in (50mm) and mark again, and repeat this from the mark on the other side. You should have four marks in total. Don't worry about the marks showing as the wire will cover them all.

2 Take the 18 gauge wire and, starting at one of the first marks up from the end of the band, wrap the wire around the band five times, so the wire coil ends on the pen mark. The long end on the 18 gauge wire needs to be where the pen mark is.

3 Measure along the 18 gauge wire about 2in (50mm) and bend the wire back toward the band. Measure another 2$\frac{1}{8}$in (53mm) and bend again. The wire will want to curve naturally so you should see an ear shape forming.

4 Place the final bend you made in step 3 under the hair band and start a coil around the band at the pen mark. Keep coiling until you get to the next pen mark. Try to keep the coil tight to the band and close together. 18 gauge wire is pretty hard so it will take some effort to make it coil nicely.

5 Repeat step 3 for the second ear.

6 Find the final pen mark and coil five times around the band. Snip off any extra wire.

7 Take the 24 gauge wire and coil a couple of times around the base of one of the cat ears.

8 Thread a few crystals onto the wire and coil around the 18 gauge wire on the opposite side of the ear. Add more crystals and coil around the opposite side again.

9 Keep adding a few crystals at a time and wrap the wire from side to side and up and down until you have a pattern you are happy with. This project used about 40 crystals per ear but you can add more or less as desired. Repeat for the other ear.

TO MAKE YOUR HAIRBAND SIT COMFORTABLY BEHIND THE EARS, BEND IT INTO A "U" SHAPE WITH YOUR FINGERS.

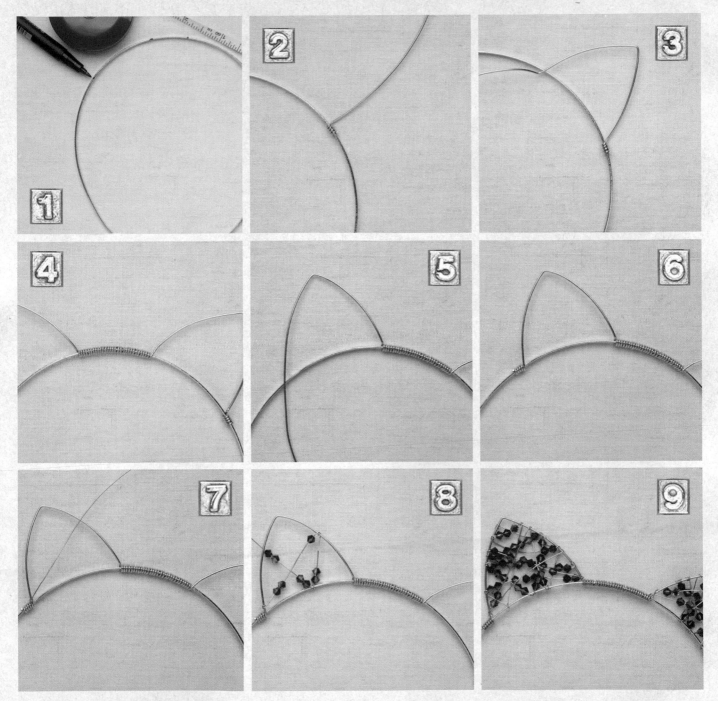

jasper

Cute tiger faces give
these pretty hair grips
some personality!

Everything you will need...

These tiger buttons are great to make any cat-loving young girl the perfect hair accessory.

1. Tiger face plastic button
2. 2in (50mm) thin orange felt
3. Polyurethane matte varnish
4. Hair clasp
5. E6000 glue
6. Black permanent marker pen

Sharp scissors

Paintbrush

Craft knife

Cutting mat or chopping board

Nonstick tile

Tracing paper

Pencil

Assembling jasper

1 Take a button and carefully cut off the back with a craft knife. Hold the button against something to brace it, such as a wooden chopping board or cutting mat.

2 Take the felt and coat with the matte varnish. This job is messy as the felt will soak up the varnish, so work on a nonstick surface like a tile. Leave to completely dry.

3 Trace the template outline onto tracing paper and cut it out. Now lay the template onto the stiffened felt and draw around the edge with a pencil. Cut the shape out with small sharp scissors.

4 Lay the felt shape down with the button centered on top. Take the marker pen and draw dots on the felt where the black stripes meet the edge on the tiger face button. The plan is to extend the black face stripes across the felt to the edge. When you have all the marks in place, remove the button and draw the black lines to the edge of the felt. Make them thicker in the middle, becoming thinner as they meet the edge of the felt.

5 Using the E6000 glue, glue the tiger face onto the front of the felt. E6000 takes a while to dry, so you have time to make sure the face is central on the felt. Leave to dry.

6 Take the hair clasp and glue the tiger face to the end using E6000 glue. The tiger can face in any direction, so before you get the glue out, take a moment to decide which way you want it to face before gluing it on.

IF YOU DON'T WANT TO PLAY AROUND WITH FELT THESE BUTTONS ALSO LOOK GREAT GLUED ON GRIPS ON THEIR OWN.

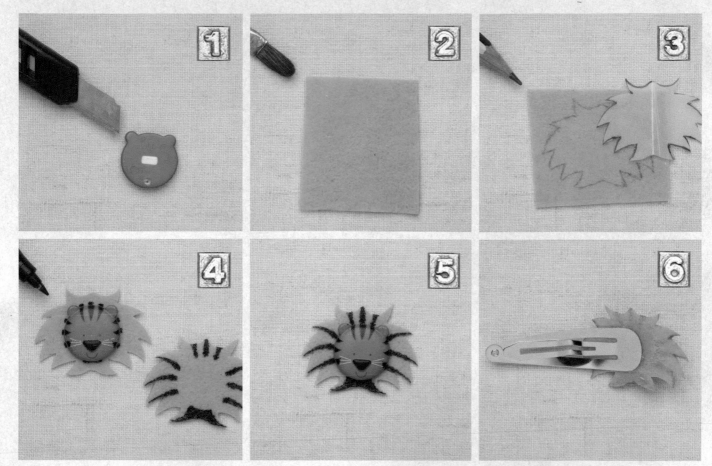

MANY ANIMAL FACE BUTTONS ARE AVAILABLE
SO WHY NOT MAKE UP A WHOLE ZOO?

athena

A line of colorful enamel
cats are stationed along
this haircomb.

Everything you will need...

Delicate cloisonné multicolored cats decorate a small comb to make a perfect party accessory.

1 5 x 17mm cloisonné cat beads

2 1 x 2in (50mm) metal haircomb

3 1 x 15in (380mm) x US 26 gauge (SWG 27, 0.4mm) silver-colored wire

Superglue

Chain-nose pliers

Side cutters

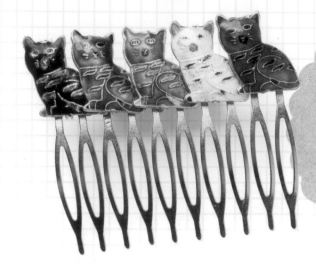

THIS PROJECT WILL WORK WELL WITH ANY STYLE OF COMB. YOU CAN USE A PLASTIC ONE IF YOU PREFER.

Assembling athena

1 Take the wire and the haircomb. Attach the wire to the comb by wrapping it around the first prong and twisting the wire together to secure it to the comb. Bring the wire back around the comb so it is sitting in-between two prongs.

2 Take a cat bead and thread it onto the wire from the bottom so the wire comes out of the head. Take the wire down the back of the cat and wrap it once around the comb, between the same prongs. Take the wire back through the bead again and down the back, bringing the wire back up in between the third and forth prongs. Add another cat bead and repeat this step to attach it securely to the comb.

3 Keep adding the cat beads following step 2, making sure the cat to the right sits in front of the one to its left.

4 When you have added the final cat bead, wrap the wire around the comb twice to secure.

5 Take the wire end and wrap it around the two wires coming down the back of the final cat bead. Coil it around a couple of times and cut the end off neatly with side cutters.

6 To make sure the cats are secure and that they don't move when being worn, go along the comb behind the cats with a small amount of superglue. Be careful when applying glue, as you don't want to flood the area.

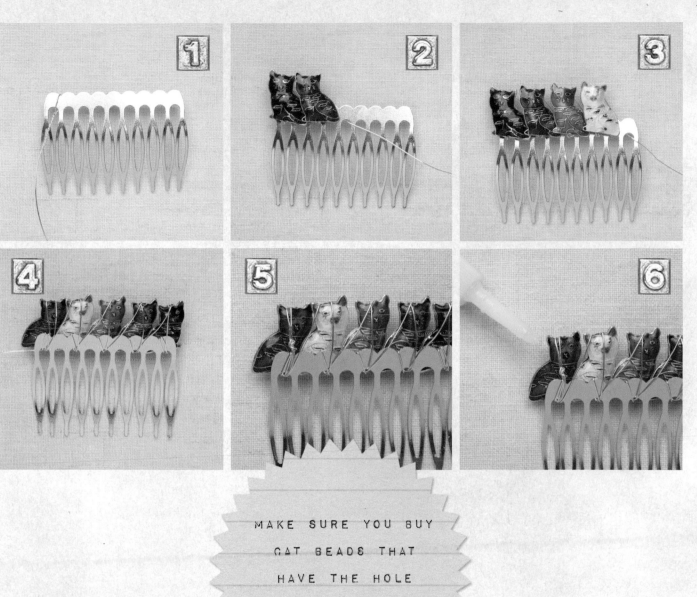

MAKE SURE YOU BUY
CAT BEADS THAT
HAVE THE HOLE
RUNNING FROM TOP
TO BOTTOM.

resources

SOURCES OF MATERIALS

UK

The Bead & Button Company
The Workshop
58 Lower North Road
Carnforth
Lancashire
LA5 9LJ
www.beadandbuttoncompany.co.uk

The Bead Merchant
PO Box 5025
Coggeshall
Essex
CO6 1HW
Tel: +44 (0)1376 570022
www.beadmerchant.co.uk

The Bead Shop
44 Higher Ardwick
Manchester
M12 6DA
Tel: +44 (0)161 2744040
www.the-beadshop.co.uk

Beads Direct Ltd
10 Duke Street
Loughborough
Leicestershire
LE11 1ED
Tel: +44 (0)1509 218028
www.beadsdirect.co.uk

Beads Unlimited
PO Box 1
Hove
East Sussex
BN3 5SG
Tel: +44 (0)1273 740777
www.beadsunlimited.co.uk

Fred Aldous Ltd
37 Lever Street
Manchester
M1 1LW
Tel: +44 (0)161 2364224
www.fredaldous.co.uk

JillyBeads
1 Anstable Road
Morecambe
LA4 6TG
Tel: +44 (0)1524 412728
www.jillybeads.co.uk

Palmer Metals Ltd
401 Broad Lane
Coventry
CV5 7AY
Tel: +44 (0)845 6449343
www.palmermetals.co.uk

Resin 8
7 Gloucester Street
Winchcombe
Gloucestershire
GL54 5LX
Tel: +44 (0)1242 602739
www.resin8.co.uk

Spoilt Rotten Beads
7 The Green
Haddenham
Ely
Cambridgeshire
CB6 3TA
Tel: +44 (0)1353 749853
www.spoiltrottenbeads.co.uk

Worldwide

Fire Mountain Gems and Beads
1 Fire Mountain Way
Grants Pass
OR 97526-2373
USA
Tel: 1-800-355-2137 (toll free in USA)
    +1-541-956-7890
www.firemountaingems.com

Shipwreck Beads
8560 Commerce Place Dr
NE Lacey
WA 98516
USA
Tel: 1-800-355-2137 (toll free in USA)
    +1-360-754-2323
www.shipwreckbeads.com

acknowledgments

I would like to say thank you to my husband for his continuing support and to Wendy McAngus for her help and guidance—we make a good team!

about the author

Sian Hamilton graduated from Brighton University in the southeast of England with a BA Honours Degree in Three-dimensional Design. She has worked in the design industry for over 20 years, working mainly in ceramics and jewelry design. Sian is currently the Editor of *Making Jewellery* magazine alongside running her own jewelry company making wedding accessories and bespoke jewelry for private clients. She is also the author of *Flowers* for GMC Publications.

index

ADDITIONAL PHOTOGRAPHY CREDITS

Soon, the Black Cat Tour by Rodolphe Salis (p29 top left); Jana-milena/Photocase.com (p47 bottom right); Jules13/Photocase.com (p64 top left); Beate-Helena/Photocase.com (p65 bottom center); Gano10/Photocase.com (p82 bottom left); Muybridge, Eadweard, 1830-1904 (p83 bottom right). Other images courtesy of Dover Publications (p46 top left, p47 top left, p64 bottom right, p65 top left, p82 top left, p83 bottom left, p100 top, p101 bottom right). Special thanks to Judy Pepper for her images of Mo (used in Polly on pages 56–59 and Star pages 102–105 and on page 100) and to David Cresswell and Gary Hall for their image of Dolly and Maud (page 100).

To place an order, or request
a catalog, contact:

GMC Publications Ltd
Castle Place, 166 High Street,
Lewes, East Sussex, BN7 1XU
United Kingdom

Tel: +44 (0)1273 488005

www.gmcbooks.com